MULL, IONA AND STAFFA

F

FRANCES LINCOLN LIMITED
PUBLISHERS

MULL, IONA AND STAFFA

Malcolm MacGregor

PAGE 1 Deserted beach near
Scoor, south coast of Mull

PREVIOUS PAGE South-east coast
of Iona in evening light

THIS PAGE Rock pool in
north Mull

Once again for Fiona and Natasha

Frances Lincoln Limited
4 Torriano Mews
Torriano Avenue
London NW5 2RZ
www.franceslincoln.com

Mull, Iona and Staffa
Copyright © Frances Lincoln Limited 2011
Text copyright © Malcolm MacGregor 2011
Illustrations copyright © Malcolm MacGregor 2011
First Frances Lincoln edition 2011

A catalogue record for this book is available from the
British Library.

ISBN 978-0-7112-2902-0

Printed and bound in China
9 8 7 6 5 4 3 2 1

Contents

Outer
Hebrides

SKYE

Inverness

MULL

SCOTLAND
Glasgow

ATLANTIC
OCEAN

NORTHERN
IRELAND

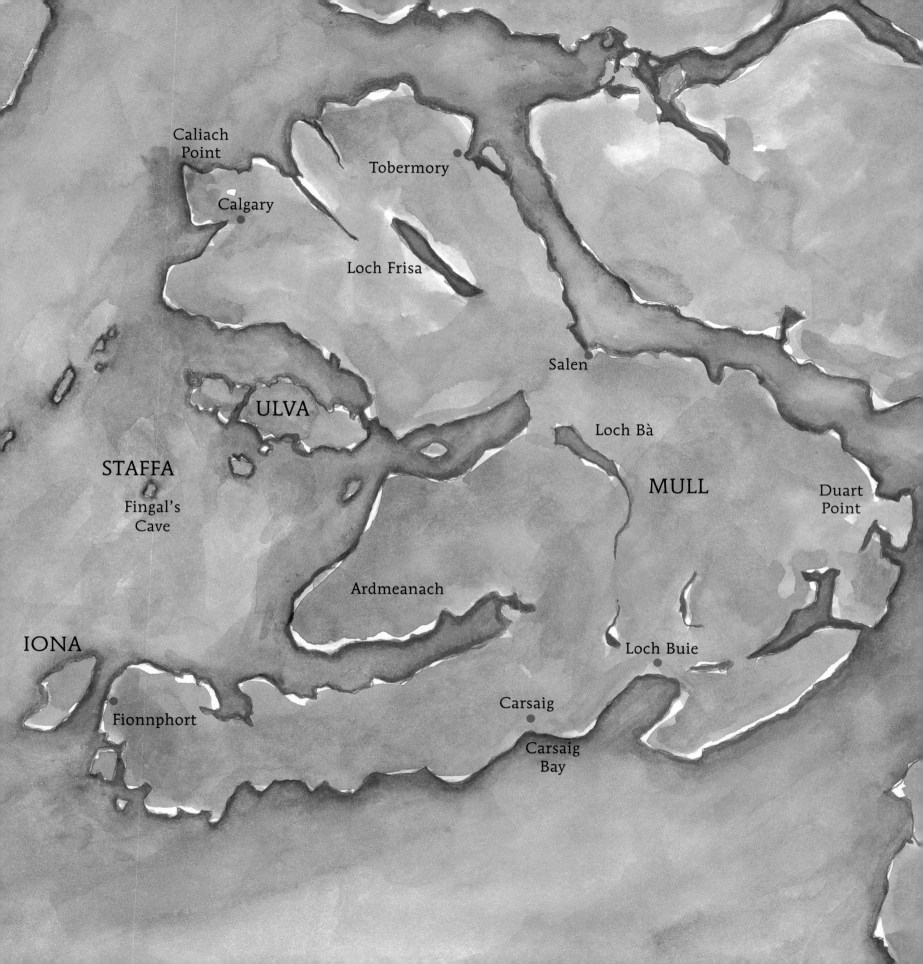

Introduction

THE THREE INNER HEBRIDEAN ISLANDS of Mull, Iona and Staffa conjure up images of barren rocky coastline with pristine shores that glisten in the sun. The populations of Mull and Iona are small, and Staffa is unoccupied, deserted long ago. Despite being close to the mainland of Argyll and Morvern to the north, the islands share a common remoteness, which locks the three of them together. Their landscape is one of big lochs, mountains and caves with some Christian spirituality thrown in.

While there are many islands that make up the Inner Hebrides, from Mingulay to Lismore, all have their own special character and beauty, and Mull, Iona and Staffa are no different. Although they are grouped together by proximity, they could not be more different. They can be deceiving, as they look as if there is not much to them. But there is, of course, a great deal.

Mull is the most prominent, its mountains and snow-capped peaks making it look very much like a part of the Highlands of Scotland. Looking across to Mull from Oban on the Argyll coast, the mountains of Ben More and A' Chioch are the primary features one sees on the distant horizon. The island seems like an extension of the mainland, except that there are 5 miles/8 kilometres of sea between it and the mainland. And therein lies Mull's story. Completely surrounded by water, its whole life has been, and still is, based around the sea, as too are the lives of Iona and Staffa.

Winter sunrise on Ben More

Mull feels as if it is in the centre of things, governing everything around it. Look east and the mainland is only 2 miles/3 kilometres away. Look west and there are many other islands – Treshnish, Staffa, Coll and Tiree. To the south are Jura, Islay and Colonsay.

I was often told on my visits to Mull that geographically and historically it should be regarded not as an appendage to the west Highlands but rather as a place with its own identity and unique qualities. For Mull has a record of historical events and towns that are as significant as anything to be found on the mainland. Its looming castles, standing stones and ancient sites remind the traveller of bygone eras, including those of clan warfare: this is an island where the clan Maclean, or Gillean, once had superiority over all others. In addition it has exotic gardens, harbours for yachts, forestry,

beaches and, perhaps its main feature, a number of waterfalls that crash into the sea, such as those on Ardmeanach, which can be seen from Iona. It has the deep sea lochs of Scridain and Loch na Keal and mighty coastal cliffs. This is an island possessed of much water, with long rivers and wet mountains. It is frequently clad in snow, despite being out at sea.

In the case of Iona it is the green and turquoise seas that give it its character, combined with its history as the site of the origin of Christianity in the Western Isles. This is the appeal for thousands of pilgrims throughout the year.

With Staffa it is the rock and the spectacular Fingal's Cave, which cuts so deeply into the island, that hold the attraction. The basalt columns inspire and give visitors much to dwell upon. Keats described Fingal's

LEFT Duart castle on Mull's eastern crags

RIGHT Sunrise on the nunnery, Iona

Cave as having greater solemnity and grandeur than the finest cathedral, and music has been set to its name. You can feel the shape and age of these rocks and contemplate the geological links to Giant's Causeway on the north coast of Ireland, and to Iceland, some 800 miles/1,200 kilometres away.

From these three islands you do not look out to a swirling ocean and ponder that the next landfall is Canada, for these are the Inner Hebrides and have a closeness to other Hebridean islands. For Staffa that proximity is to the Treshnish Isles; from Iona it is Staffa, and of course Mull; from Mull it is Coll, Tiree, Jura and Islay and the small isles of Rùm, Canna and Eigg. There is no sense of isolation here, as might be found in the Outer Hebrides, though there are isolated and lonely settings.

My aim in this book is not to give a detailed description of relics and artefacts (there are plenty of guide books which do that) but to describe what it is like to be here and experience the islands in all weathers and at varying times of year. Like many locations, they are best seen when one is alone on the moorland, or on some solitary beach with nothing but the incessant washing of surf on sand to break the silence. My purpose is to reveal through photography some of the more secluded and unusual aspects of the islands. I wanted to be well off the beaten track and get into the heartland of Mull; I hoped to delve deep around the coast of Iona and go beyond Fingal's Cave on Staffa.

Trekking up steep ridgelines for a dawn photograph of Ben More in winter and in summer was part of my

quest to find sights with meaning. And in order to seek out the unusual aspects, lengthy walks were required, like the one to the Carsaig Arches on the south coast of Mull, or the walk to Port na Curaich on the south coast of Iona over the hills from Baille Mor, the main town, which takes a good hour in daylight, longer when returning in darkness. There is something revelatory as the light is fading; a chill wind gets up and the light gives way gradually to complete darkness; it is when one can hear the waves but not see them.

The Hebrides have always been well known for their light, but Mull, Iona and Staffa have their own special quality. In order to capture it I often visited the same place twice. I cannot count the number of storms I endured, but perversely I came to learn that storms were my friend and not a hindrance to photography. They gave notice that spectacular light was coming and I had better get ready, for once they had cleared it was remarkable to see the light displayed across the sea and on the land. Sometimes I did miss the drama of unfolding colour, but I also learnt that to appreciate these islands you don't always have to photograph them.

ABOVE Storm-struck pink granite rock, south Mull

RIGHT Loch Buie in a storm

MULL

'Mull of the sweet singers and of the green woods, there is no island of the west that can compare with you in calm restful beauty.'

SETON GORDON

North Mull

AS AN ISLAND LANDSCAPE MULL has its own dramatic and intense identity. It is mountainous, with the only Hebridean Munro, Ben More, at 3,170 feet/966 metres. This is fairly central and can be climbed and admired from both north and south. The major sea loch is Loch na Keal which, like its counterpart in the south, Loch Scridain, cuts deep into east coast of the island. Like neighbouring Iona and Staffa, the rock is mainly volcanic.

Heading north from the main ferry terminal, Craignure, is Salen, an old town with an immediate reminder of the island's fishing heritage: two old fishing vessels marooned on the shore. The wind whips across their decks from the Morvern hills on the mainland and the Sound of Mull 2 miles/3 kilometres away.

Northwards up the coast is the striking port of Tobermory. The Gaelic rendition of its name is Tobar Mhoire, meaning 'St Mary's well'. The town was built by

PREVIOUS PAGES Calgary Bay

LEFT Nets in Tobermory

LEFT Tobermory house

BELOW Tobermory distillery

the 5th Duke of Argyll and the British Fisheries Society in 1788. Much has been written about Tobermory; it has been described as the finest small town in the Hebrides and it certainly lives up to the praise. It has an almost perfect circular bay and its colourful row of shorefront houses embracing shades of blue, pink, red and orange add real character. Among discarded fishing nets are bookshops, galleries, coffee shops and restaurants. For sailors it is one of the most secure anchorages. The island's main distillery is located here, having been founded in 1798. Despite numerous closures and re-openings it is now a going concern, producing both a blend and a malt whisky.

About a half-hour walk north of Tobermory along a ragged path above the cliffs is the lighthouse at Rubha nan Gall. This is the only sign of man's

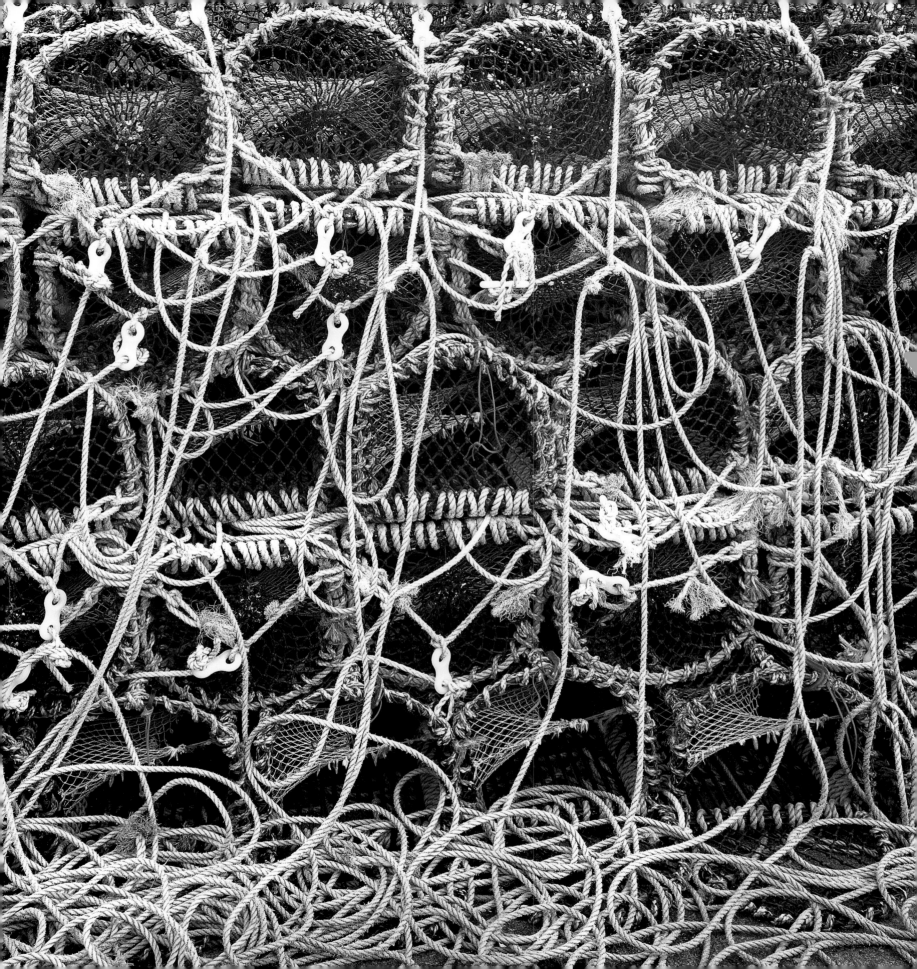

BELOW Caliach Point
on the north coast of
Mull, with the hills of
Rùm across the sea

RIGHT Lighthouse at Rubha nan Gall, with Ben Hiant on the mainland in the distance

work on a barren headland with outstanding views to the hills of Ardnamurchan on the mainland. A walkway leads out to the lighthouse, whose presence is a reminder of the violent seas and storm-ridden coastline that sailors must beware of, for there are no harbours or sheltered points up here – only names from the distant past, such as Bloody Bay, site of a sea battle among the Macdonalds.

Caliach Point is the most north-western extremity on Mull, accessible by track from Calgary. The island has many promontories, where seals sun themselves and fulmars dart in and out of the rocks. On a clear day at Caliach, views to the north take in Rùm and the Ardnamurchan lighthouse, the most westerly point on the mainland. Far in the distance the Cuillins of Skye can be identified by their volcanic, jagged, black outline. Like many a headland Caliach is isolated and exposed,

with only one farmhouse near by. All else is windswept moorland and steep cliffs.

Calgary, or in Gaelic Caladh Garaidh, means 'haven by the dyke'. The name is perhaps more famous as that of the biggest town in Alberta, Canada, which is renowned for its annual stampede or rodeo. The story goes that a Colonel Macleod of the Canadian Mounted Police so enjoyed a holiday at Calgary that on his return to Canada in 1883 he gave the city the same name. Calgary in Mull is well positioned, overlooking a white sandy beach and attractive inlet, with the island of Coll shimmering on the distant horizon.

Following the coast in a south-westerly direction you come to the deserted village of Crackaig, which was 'cleared' of its 200 inhabitants in the nineteenth century. Such villages appear to be lifeless, as all that remains are empty shells that were formerly houses.

Turquoise sea, Ulva

But often there is an evocative mood: you look at them knowing that families once made their lives there, albeit pretty arduous ones.

From Crackaig the eye is drawn westwards across the sea to Dutchman's Cap, Staffa and Ulva. Ulva means 'wolf island' in old Norse, and access is by ferry from just beyond the schoolhouse at Oskamull. Very few people live on the island and, like other places, it has changed ownership many times over the years. Ulva was home to the Macquaries, whose most famous descendant, General Lachlan Macquarie, became the first Governor General of New South Wales in Australia and one of the founding fathers of that country. Because of debts, Ulva passed out of the hands of the Macquarie clan in 1777, but they managed to repurchase it for a short period in 1825 until it had to be sold again. Another notable descendant of the island was the African explorer and missionary Dr David Livingstone, whose grandfather was a crofter.

As at Crackaig, the islanders suffered during the Clearances, when the island population was reduced from 500 to just 150. The ruined village of Ormaig, which looks straight across to the Gribun escarpment of Mull, was home to many families. After the potato famine of 1848 most of these families were 'cleared' to distant parts of the world. Remnants of the houses still stand, among trickling streams from which the occupants would have drawn their water.

Camping here overnight was a sublime experience: the sound of falling water mixed with the melodious calls of a cuckoo, which complimented the ambience of last light, as fine reflections off the sea took on a translucent glow in the darkening night. The dim basalt crags were a reminder of Staffa and the fault line that leads to it, while the outline of Inchkenneth, once the island home of the eccentric Mitford family, could just be discerned.

Loch na Keal, meaning 'loch of the cliff', is the major sea loch in the north of Mull and its long shoreline contributes 15 miles/24 kilometres to the extensive 300 miles/480 kilometres of coastline that encircles the island. Along its shores and among the bluffs are dark tangled woods of oak and beech along with myriad rock formations, many of which have settled into the shape of the loch over the years.

Close to Loch na Keal is the secluded Loch Bà, which nestles among the hills and glens between Ben More and Salen. A walk along its shores takes you deep into

LEFT Bracken and snow illuminated by evening light leading to Ben nan Gabhar

ABOVE Evening light on Loch na Keal

the heart of Mull and to the foot of Cruachan Beg and Cruachan Dearg, prominent tops within this mountain range. Most of the shoreline is wooded and autumn is a fine time to be here, when ambient colours reflect off the surface of the loch.

On the north shore of Loch na Keal is what could be referred to as the Ben More massif, a range of hills that are centred around this Munro. Each has its own name, and a good way of identifying them is from the north side, where they roll into each other to help form the 3,170 feet/966 metres of the mountain. Being among these hills in winter has its own enchantment. I decided to photograph Ben More from nearby Ben Fhada after a somewhat lengthy assessment of the lie of the land. Ben Fhada would, in my estimation, give me a good angle of view on to the mountain, particularly at dawn. Setting off in the clear night at 5.00 a.m. from the loch, I headed through boggy scrubland until I encountered the first of a series of uphill scrambles, and then a second ledge and a third and fourth. By 7.00

a.m. it was just getting light enough to find my way without a torch, and I could move faster and skirt round iced-up pools and frozen rocks. By 7.45 a.m. I was on a ledge on Ben Fhada with a stunning view across to the mountain.

All was clear and still. Cloud was swirling around the summit and I was fearful that there would be no exposure of it. But once I had got the camera set up, the cloud dissipated for sunrise and there was a light pinkish hue on the top. This was roughly what I was looking for. I could feel a sense of grandeur about the mountain but no mystery; perhaps the light was too clear and there were no clouds to diffuse it. Nonetheless, the silence was so intense that every step spoke loudly as I crunched through the snow and ice. This was

perfection, with no rain lashing down, just the ice-cold image of Ben More with snow-clad glens and rivers falling away from the mountain. Looking back down on my route I could see the great Loch na Keal and its amazing crooked shape, with a well-defined Ulva and Gometra to the north.

Beyond Gribun at the entrance to Loch na Keal is the Ardmeanach peninsula, or 'the wilderness', as it is sometimes known. This coastal landscape is on a grand scale, comparable to Torridon in the north-west Highlands. Ardmeanach is also characterized by its well-displayed lava flows from fifty million years ago, which have been weathered into terraces and may be seen distinctly from the south shore of Loch Scridain.

The easiest way in to the peninsula is from the

RIGHT Autumn colours
reflected in Loch Bà

BELOW Beech tree on Loch Bà

National Trust car park just beyond Tiroran House. From here it is a two-hour hike along a good track before it eventually becomes a footpath. The track is reasonably well elevated, looking down on Loch Scridain to the south, with Iona shimmering on the horizon. Leaving signs of life behind at Tavool there is great feeling of being in a remote wilderness, despite being on an island. The track becomes a footpath at a place called Burg, where Chrissie MacGillivray once lived, dispensing tea to walkers intent on seeing this outstanding piece of coastline. She was the last in a line of MacGillivrays who lived and worked in this inaccessible spot. Burg and its acres of rocky outcrops, scree and caves is now owned by the National Trust for Scotland. The land around Burg is characterized by memorial cairns to Chrissie, her brother Duncan and Daisy Cheape, a little girl who drowned in Loch Scridain in 1896. These cairns are evidence of a once vibrant life: a community life one would not believe, given the sheer isolation of the place. While from a distance Ardmeanach can look wild, to these inhabitants it was home, and they adapted to its harsh beauty.

Beyond Burg the footpath descends steeply to the coast; the rocks become blacker, basalt is more in evidence and the wind increases. Rounding the point, the path climbs upwards to a red-rocked boulder field, which must once have been part of the cliff. Herds of deer are sometimes seen down by the sea, along with wild goats. The ocean is clear, with an almost mercurial

light to it in the setting sun. Here there is a real feeling of space across the wide expanse of sea. Huge waterfalls plunge into the sea; after an incessant spell of rain they can be seen from Iona. When the sun dips to the horizon the boulders are illuminated for a few minutes only and the whole face comes alive with light. This is the famed Hebridean light. Then it suddenly dies as the sun disappears, leaving an orange line across the sea's horizon. The strange afterglow gives the water the appearance of shifting mercury. The sight is captivating, as a certain luminosity moves back and forth across the surface in the half-glow of the dwindling light. But it is a long walk back to Tiroran in the dark over boulders and through bracken, making it easy to miss the line of the track.

Mull is one of the few places where one can experience the full force of inclement weather followed by extraordinary light. The power of light and the sight of storms forming and moving over the Minch (the channel between the mainland and the Hebrides) like some supernatural force is mesmerizing. You can see the band of the storm circling far out over the Dutchman's Cap, moving with intent over Staffa and then driving itself headlong for Mull. As soon as you feel the first drops of rain on the camera it is time to pack it away, because within seconds the full force of the storm is upon you. The noise can be deafening, like the cracks of a thousand bullets. Then minutes later it eases and

ABOVE Rock face above
Loch na Keal

the rain loses its intensity and slowly moves on. Within moments you can look seawards and experience the luminescence that comes behind the storm. This is something I have not seen elsewhere, except perhaps in the Outer Hebrides, which are famed for the pure Atlantic light. But there it is different – less intense. Off Mull it has a clear brilliance that defines the islands and rocks and the sea horses being blown towards the shore. The sea changes colour from dark to light blue with an emerald tinge before your eyes. Then another storm beckons, moving over Staffa, and it is time to wrap up yet again and endure the noise and the drenching, before the shroud of light returns. The experience is intensified by the realization that what you have witnessed may well be unshared, as there is no one for miles – not even a trawler.

South Mull

WHILE THE NORTH has Ben More and the wilderness country of Ardmeanach, the southern coastline of Mull has its own uniqueness. It is a revelation of sheer drops, arches and pink granite rock on a grand scale. There are lonely walks along escarpments, where no one lives, and only the alternating sea colour for company and to captivate the senses. While Iona with its abbey can claim a spiritual and religious history, Mull claims a different narrative. Its castles and glens witnessed the fighting between warring clans, predominantly sea-based Scots who raided far and wide, including the mainland of Scotland and Ireland. In the southern part of the island the castle of Duart, meaning 'black point', and the castle of Moy on Loch Buie are testimony to clan life.

Duart Castle is home to the chiefs of Clan Maclean, and is one of the most iconic locations in the whole of Scotland. Sitting on a strategic corner of Mull it commands the sea routes into Loch Linnhe, Loch Etive, the Firth of Lorne and the Sound of Mull. Who cannot be moved by the sight of it, as it comes into view from the ferry on the approach to Craignure? Who cannot wonder at its history and its role in former times? It is the epitome of what visitors from abroad imagine Scotland to be and it does not disappoint.

RIGHT Dawn over Duart Bay

The story of the Macleans cannot really be told without the story of Duart Castle.

There are many castles on the west coast of Scotland that lie ruined and have never been restored – Aros on Mull is an example; Ardtornish and Dunollie on the mainland are two more. It is therefore surprising and heartening to see a castle that has been restored to its former glory and is lived in by the chief of the clan, Sir Lachlan Maclean of Duart and Morvern. For hundreds of years the castle was an empty shell, overgrown with bracken and grass. It had been destroyed by Clan Campbell after the Jacobite uprising of 1688 and passed into the hands of the Duke of Argyll, the Campbell chief. Although occupied by government troops until 1750, after this date the fortification became dilapidated. It was not until 1911 that the then clan chief, Sir Fitzroy Maclean, aged seventy, bought back Duart Point and the remains of the castle. Employing the Scottish architect Sir John Burnett, he set about returning it to its former glory. This took energy and imagination,

but by 1912 the chief was back in his stronghold, and Macleans gathered from all over the world to celebrate the restoration. Clansmen and women came from as far afield as America and Australia – well before the advent of passenger airlines.

Since 1912 the Macleans have assembled in Mull many times, and like their forebears in 1912 they come from all over the world. They are a big clan with many members and descendants. Their patronymic is 'Gillean'; hence the name Maclean, meaning 'son of Gillean'. Their first chief was Gillean of the battleaxe, who descended from the kings of Dalriada, the ancient kingdom of Scotland founded at Dunadd in Argyll. His descendants were many and the name Maclean is practically synonymous with Mull. In fact the clan is so big that there are Macleans of Ardgour and Drimin on the mainland and on Mull there are Macleans from Brolas, Calgary, Torloisk and Pennycross. There is even a branch of the clan in Sweden. There is another local branch with its own chief, based around Loch Buie; they use a different spelling – Maclaine.

The Macleans were a major sea-borne race. They were the pre-eminent clan in Mull and its surrounding islands, comparable to the Macneils of Barra in the Outer Hebrides. One of the chiefs married a daughter of the Lord of the Isles, acquiring vast tracks of land in Mull, so that he was able to bear the Viking black galley on his flag. It was he who commanded the war fleets on behalf of the Lord of the Isles that sailed the high seas as far as Loch Foyle in Ireland.

While the Macleans were in conflict with other clans

LEFT Killean graveyard with Ben Buie in the distance

RIGHT Loch Buie stone circle

such as the Mackinnons and Maclaines of Loch Buie, their main enemy was the Argyll-based Clan Campbell. The height of conflict was at the time of the Jacobite uprisings, as the Campbells supported the victorious government side. They captured and destroyed Duart Castle, thereby winning control of most of Mull, along with the sea approaches. A landownership map of Mull from 1700 shows the Campbells of Argyll owning most of the island, with the Mackinnons holding a small part of the north and the Macleans an area to the south. There are still a fair number of Campbells living on the island to this day. A wander through any of the old graveyards will reveal many Highland names. One such is that at remote Killean, overlooking Loch Spelve. Originally the only way there was by sea,

but today you can reach it by an hour's walk from the main road across the hills.

A more peaceful setting is nearby Torosay gardens, which also look out to Duart Bay. These gardens and the accompanying castle are owned and run as a private enterprise. Taking advantage of the warm Atlantic weather and the Gulf Stream, the gardens were created by Murray Guthrie in 1900 and today his great-grandson Christopher James has expanded and developed them on a magnificent scale. Paths lead from cedars to rhododendrons, creating a mix of the exotic and colourful in a place of outstanding beauty.

Mull is the principal island among surrounding ones such as Ulva, Inchkenneth, Staffa, Gometra and Iona and it was to Mull that the inhabitants of these islands

looked. In order to get cattle to the mainland and ultimately to the trysts at Crieff and Falkirk, they had to pass through Mull. The drove roads on Mull led to Grass Point, where cattle gathered before onward transportation to the mainland. Pilgrims going in the other direction to Iona made use of Grass Point, probably landing there amidst huge herds of cattle waiting to be transported across the Firth of Lorn to Kerrera. The old ferry site can still be seen today.

A fork in the road at Ardura leads south to Loch Buie, a distant sea loch at the end of the great glen fault. It is a barren and windy spot, lying in the shadow of its cousin, Ben Buie, which means 'yellow hill'. Loch Buie itself comprises a village, a large house and the remains of Moy Castle. The loch is at the end of the road and forceful gales that have assembled out in the Minch blow straight up the loch, whipping the sea into a frenzy, while tempestuous waves strike the shore without respite.

About 2 miles/3 kilometres to the south of the village along the shore, in a majestic setting overlooked by surrounding hills, stands a mausoleum that was converted from a chapel to a burial place for the chiefs of the Maclaines of Lochbuie in 1864. Inside are some old gravestones and wall plaques, but the harsh weather and barrenness give it a melancholy feel.

There are many standing stones on Mull, as there are throughout the Hebrides. The most impressive is a stone circle in a field in the shadow of Ben Buie. The approach is fairly easy if you follow some white stones. Why this stone circle, which consists of eight stones and a couple near by, is located here is not really known. But Loch Buie is easily accessible by sea, and the mountain would have been a good lookout point.

Leaving the circle and setting out along the track on the north side of the loch, you eventually come to the remote and isolated Carsaig Bay. The walk – a distance of about 5 miles/8 kilometres – is hard going over broken ground, interspersed with large rocks and a track that disappears in and out of these black volcanic rocks at various points; the sea air is fresh but can turn violent quickly, so good protection and boots are essential. But the reward is a picturesque sight: Carsaig means 'curled bay' in old Norse, and here are the remains of a solid old pier, a boathouse and a couple of cottages. There are spectacular views across the rock flats to Jura, Islay and Colonsay. Often there are otters playing in the sea off the pier.

Pressing on, the route below the bluffs leads eventually to the Carsaig Arches below Malcolm's Point. The hike is about 4 miles/6 kilometres across broken ground, with scattered flotsam from the sea – buoys, plastic bottles, great planks of wood – and carcases of deer, which have tumbled off the towering cliffs above. Black volcanic rocks and huge boulders impede progress but add to the feeling of being alone. The arches appear after about 4 miles/6 kilometres. As you descend the ridge, one arch becomes visible, standing proud against the sea, while the other is tucked away. Both are made of columnar basalt, with wide cave-like openings that have been bored out by the incessant thrashing of the waves in high winds. To find such a geological spectacle in such a far-flung location is a great reward for one's effort. This is Mull at its best: a place where you feel you are at the end of the earth, with the entrances to the arches looking as if they lead to another planet.

While Iona and Staffa possess little vegetation, Mull has an array of oak and beech trees with hazel, iris and rowan in profusion. On the road from Carsaig north to Loch Scridain there is a good example: on the brow of a hill looking down on the loch is a line of beech trees and Scots pines. Towering in the distance is the outline of Ben More. In winter, snowstorms can be seen driving into the tops of Ben More and A' Chioch. The road falls to the loch and a sharp turn to the right leads along the shoreline to Pennyghael and on to the head

of Loch Scridain and the mouth of the Coladoir River.

The Coladoir is a spate river that flows through the hills, collecting the water and snowmelt that flow off Ben Buie. The water cuts its way to the sea, forcing itself through big red boulders into gullies and small canyons. The force, particularly in winter, causes fine clouds of spray and little rainbows against the caverns. Clambering around the boulders one can feel encased by the Ben More massif, Ben Buie and the tops of Corra Ben and Cruachan Dearg.

Mull cannot really be experienced without getting up high and while Ben More is an outstanding island Munro, the surrounding hills are also inviting, particularly as there are old sheep tracks up burns. This is the beauty of Mull: hidden gems of landscape; a waterfall here; an isolated rock pool there; glistening aquamarine water in a burn up some lonely glen – for anyone who desires intimacy with the landscape, it is perfect.

Heading west along Loch Scridain above the shore, with Ardmeanach on the distant skyline, you eventually

BELOW Sunlit tops and ice
pool from Corra Ben

RIGHT South face of Ben More
at sunrise

come to the town of Bunessan, where the old Glasgow steamer *Dunara* used to call. From here it is worth taking a detour south to the Scoor escarpment. The route skirts round the back of Scoor farm and, following a track, bypasses the remains of Shiaba, where at the end of the eighteenth century some 300 people lived. The track hugs the tree line of a plantation and soon you are at the top of the cliffs, looking down the face on to a rough and lively coastline. Another detour about 1 mile/1.5 kilometres west of the farm leads to the

white sandy beach and rocks around Port Bheathain. The morning light strikes the rocks here with a brilliance not seen in many places. Sea stacks come alive in the light before it passes over them and leaves them lifeless, save for swirling surf.

Going west along the Ross of Mull, you can sense Iona approaching, and the departure point for this holy island creeping nearer. The bustling village of Fionnphort is at the end of the road among rocks and sandy beaches. The campsite here is idyllic, and

The Coladoir river with Corra Ben and Cruachan Dearg in the distance

useful for discovering this part of the Ross. Before heading for Iona it is worth exploring the land around the old fishing village of Kintra and its line of houses where nothing moves save for the odd flock of sheep. Passing between the houses and the sea you come to Mull's famed pink granite rock. Much of it was used for Britain's buildings; the Holborn viaduct in London and Liverpool docks owe their existence to it. Sadly it is not exported any more: the costs are too great.

But for the photographer or wanderer that is good news, as the rock provides one of the most enigmatic coastlines anywhere in Britain. It is comparable to the famous pink granite rock formations around the coastal town of Perros-Guirec in Brittany. With an ever-changing light this is an inscrutable and spellbinding place. Great pink and red slabs plunge into the sea, making coloured reflections and unusual tones of colour. Crossing to Iona is an easy ten-minute ride on the ferry. As the distance from Mull increases, these masterful rock slabs are still easily discernible, standing out in contrast to the aquamarine sea and azure sky; it is a rare sight.

LEFT Beech tree near
Pennyghael

BELOW Cedar tree at Torosay

FOLLOWING PAGES
Cliffs at Scoor

ABOVE Cliffs on the south
coast near Port Bheathain

RIGHT Rock pool

ABOVE Gorge in the
Coladoir river

ABOVE RIGHT Rocks in a burn
tumbling off Ben More

FAR RIGHT Waterfalls

LEFT Ruins of old pink granite house

BELOW Thrifts growing in pink granite rock

BOTTOM Wild irises

BELOW Evening light on pink
granite rock, west coast of
Mull in the distance

RIGHT Pink granite coastline

Sunlit rocks in the Minch off
the south coast of Mull

IONA

Seven years before the Judgement,
The sea shall sweep over Erin at one tide,
And over blue-green Islay;
But the island of Columba
Shall swim above the flood.

Iona

IONA, OR IOGH AS IT USED TO BE KNOWN in Gaelic until the eighteenth century, lies at the western extremity of the Ross of Mull. Another name given to the island was I Calum Cille, 'the island of St Columba's church', in recognition of its most famous resident. Columba's Gaelic name Calum, or Calaman, means 'the dove', but he was a warrior of renown. Most people approach Iona from the Ross of Mull and there are plenty of good viewpoints across the Sound of Iona from the coastline around Fionnphort, the embarkation point for the island. From a distance Iona appears rather nondescript: fairly flat apart from a solitary hill (Dun I) and with some distinctive white beaches. However, on the approach there is a sure feeling of ancientness – of times that go back well beyond the old kings of Scotland. Iona is at the end of a pilgrimage route similar to that of Santiago de Compostela in northern Spain but much older.

The short ferry journey across the emerald-coloured Sound of Iona leads the traveller or pilgrim to one of the most iconic centres of Christianity the world has ever known. It was founded by St Columba. He did not take the same easy route to Iona; nor, indeed, did he come directly from Ireland, the land of his birth and upbringing. It is believed that this Irish prince followed a more tortuous way from Ireland up the coast of Islay to Colonsay, and then across to Iona – in effect island-hopping his way across the Irish Sea in a sail-driven *currach*, accompanied by twelve dedicated companions. They landed on the south coast in AD 563 on a shingle beach known in Gaelic as Port na Curaich.

Having confirmed his location as being on the island of Iogh, St Columba established his monastery and centre for Christian life. It is believed that the *currach* was buried where Columba and his followers landed, so they must have walked across this marshy wet land, over some hills with splendid views to the west of the raging Atlantic, where they might have seen waves crashing on to the strand at Camas Cuil an t-Saimh, which means in English the 'bay at the back of the ocean'. This is a beautiful sickle cove that is dotted with rocks among an ever-changing sea colour of blue and green.

Iona, as it came to be known (because of a mis-spelling in a document), was probably some sort of religious centre even before St Columba's arrival; certainly the island was in the charge of St Oran until he died in AD 550. Nor was St Columba the first mission-ary to promote Christianity in Scotland, for St Ninian had arrived in Galloway from Ireland well before, though his influence was confined to the south of Scotland and northern England. Nonetheless, St Columba's activities and influence were more far reaching. His mission was to convert the Picts to Christianity – a task that appears to have had mixed results over some thirty years until he died in AD 597. But from the small island of Iona, Christianity did eventually spread, via a network of churches, throughout the north of Scotland. Its growth was probably due more to those who came after St Columba and were inspired by him, rather than the impetus of the warrior-monk himself. However, he personally converted King Brude,

the Pictish king near Inverness, which was no small achievement given the dangers and distance involved. Additionally Alistair Moffat suggests in his book *The Sea Kingdoms* that St Columba's influence extended westwards to Iceland, where there is a church dedicated to him called Kolumkilli, which in Gaelic translates to Calum Cille. This was an extraordinary achievement, given that his original base was nothing more than a few caves on a small and bleak island. Perhaps most importantly, though, Iona became established as a centre in Scotland for Christian worship, life and learning, which encouraged many pilgrims to visit, and as a place for many kings to be buried.

The monastery was built in a reasonably well-protected location: from the west it was sheltered by a small hill, Dun I, and to the east by the Sound of Iona. Despite this, the descendants of St Columba were no match for the marauding Vikings who attacked the island and the monks at various intervals between 795 and 985. A few years prior to this they had struck at Lindisfarne off the Northumberland coast, so by 795 they had a taste for raiding ecclesiastical outposts of northern Europe. For the Vikings the sea was their highway to the west coast of Scotland, and Iona was on their route to the Western Isles. Despite its ferocity during intemperate weather the Atlantic was no guardian for the monks of Iona, as the names of the beaches reflect: Martyr's Bay to the south of the main jetty and to the

FAR LEFT The abbey on Iona.
with well and footbath in
the foreground

LEFT Detail of pink
granite rock used to
build the nunnery

north, one whose Gaelic name translates as 'the white strand of the monks'. In both locations the Vikings, or the 'sons of death', as they became known, massacred the resident monks and laid waste to the island.

The ruined monastery, or abbey, was reconstructed under the direction of Reginald, Lord of the Isles, a Macdonald chieftain and son of Somerled, in 1203. Little of what Reginald built remains today and most of the abbey dates from the late fifteenth century, made of granite from Tormore on the Ross of Mull, near Fionnphort.

Close by is the nunnery, which was also built by Reginald, and his sister, Bethoc, who became the first abbess. The ruins of this can be seen in their distinctive pink granite, with intricate layering of rocks and stones, among wild flowers. The stones give off an incredible glow, which feels warm even in the cold light of dawn. A nunnery would not have pleased St Columba, as he did not permit women on the island, or indeed cows, allegedly saying, 'Where there is a cow there is a woman, and where there is a woman there is mischief.'

Near the abbey is the twelfth-century St Oran's Chapel, named after the man who established a Christian sanctuary here before Columba. This was the burial place of the Lords of the Isles. These were powerful warlords of Clan Donald. Such was the sanctity of Iona that they were interred here in Oran's burial ground

RIGHT Entrance to St Oran's chapel, burial place of the Lords of the Isles

FAR RIGHT St Martin's Cross

alongside Scottish, Irish and Norwegian kings. No wonder the chapel is one of the most sacred locations in the British Isles, and the oldest ecclesiastical building on Iona.

Between the abbey and St Oran's Chapel is the magnificent and lichen-covered St Martin's Cross, which dates from around 800 AD and is over 13 feet/4 metres high. This single Celtic cross, which dominates the grounds, is a very impressive piece of early Christian carving, depicting scenes from the Old Testament.

St Columba left an incredible Christian legacy, which is shown by the large numbers of visitors who come to Iona every year. Approximately half a million of them make their way down the single-track road on the Ross of Mull. Most want to see the abbey and its surrounds, but off the beaten track and further afield they find an array of unspoilt beaches, astonishing rock formations and brightly coloured seas that are some of the finest in the Hebrides. Port Ban is a glistening green inlet that faces the Atlantic. The north coast, near the White Strand of the Monks, consists of striking rock constellations that lead the eye back to Mull and out to Staffa.

For the more inquisitive and intrepid, there are various interesting sights to see here. Not surprisingly, Iona has a spiritual quality to it that is borne out in its pure beaches, clean air and feeling of freshness. Cars are not permitted (except for those of some residents) and to get around the island you have to walk. It is an extremely well-kept place, cared for by its small population of 120. Roads and tracks, such as they are, are well looked after. The walker can make the trek to the south of the island in the opposite direction to that which St Columba and his followers took. Upon crossing the machair and the golf course, you hear great waves thumping into the caverns on the west coast where monks under the tutelage of St Columba walked 800 years before Bannockburn, the battle at which it is believed the Scottish army carried the relics of St Columba, as if believing the warrior-monk could spur them on, even in death. When you get out of sight of houses and farms there is nothing but the Atlantic and storm-ridden skies. Many visitors feel as they have been taken back hundreds of years to those primeval times, and can sense that here were the earnest beginnings of Christianity before it spread to the mainland.

West coast of Iona in
a spring gale

Another absorbing location is the disused marble quarry on the south-east coast. From here marble was shipped all over the world until the First World War. The site is accessible only through good navigation on a track that branches off from St Columba's beach. A descent via a small glen with crags on either side leads to the remains of an old bothy. This is where the quarrymen lived. It is easy to get disorientated and the bothy is the marker for the quarry, which is just to the south on another steep descent leading to the sea. Within this second narrow gully you can see the gas engine and cutting machine; just beyond are the remains of white quarried rock and an old landing post with the iron staves still in position. It is a lonely and eerie place, but among all this are impressive boulders and tones of grey, lime green, jet black and white that catch the eye. The only sound is that of stones being washed up and sucked out to sea again in the interminable movement of the ocean. If you are seeking complete solitude this is the place to come, as the quarry is difficult to find; no one will disturb you. You can rootle around on the rocks, taking in their shapes and hues, or sit on the landing point and watch the breakers strike the coast of Mull in what look like puffs of smoke.

FOLLOWING PAGES
Dark rocks on the
north coast of Iona

LEFT Glistening turquoise sea
at Port Ban

ABOVE Red rocks at Port Ban,
on the west coast

RIGHT The north coast of Iona,
with Dutchman's Cap in
the distance

STAFFA

'Staffa's isle where nature scoffs at Art!'

ANON.

Staffa

STAFFA SEEMS TO HAVE BEEN regarded over the years as one of the most exceptional of all the Hebridean islands – not because of the grandeur of any mountain or its size, but because of its basalt rock caves and hexagonal columns on sheer cliffs, which have intrigued and mesmerized people for centuries. Volcanic activity millions of years ago links Staffa to Giant's Causeway on the north coast of Ireland, where the patterns of rock are almost identical. On Staffa you can see the columnar basalt that is also a feature of the Carsaig Arches and the shoreline of the Ardmeanach peninsula on Mull in its varying colours of black, light brown and green. The blacker the basalt, the purer it is.

Staffa means 'stave island' and the pillars look like upright logs from the trees used by the Vikings to build their houses. The very name of Staffa is a reminder of the widespread Nordic influence in Scotland. Similar names in the west include Dunstaffanage (a mix of Gaelic and Norse), near Oban, and Staffin, on the Isle of Skye. Close by Viking Staffa are small rocky islands that have Gaelic names such as Am Buchaille, meaning 'the herdsman'. The mix of Norse and Gaelic is a romantic aspect of many of the place names in the Western Isles.

PREVIOUS PAGES Stormlit island of Staffa from Mull

RIGHT Basalt rock face, Staffa

Many artists, poets, musicians and composers have visited this island – Sir Walter Scott, John Keats, Felix Mendelssohn, J.M.W. Turner, William Wordsworth, Robert Louis Stevenson, to name but a few. And, of course, Queen Victoria and Prince Albert.

The island's main feature is its many caves: Boat Cave, Mackinnon's Cave, Goat Cave, Clamshell Cave, Cormorant's Cave and – the most accessible and renowned – Fingal's Cave. This is named after Fionn MacCool, an Irish warrior hero whose Gaelic name was Fingal. It has impressed artists and composers for many years. Mendelssohn wrote his Hebrides Overture ('Fingal's Cave') because he was moved by it. Painters have made it look like a Greek temple, rendering the basalt pillars to resemble columns from the Parthenon in Athens. There is an extraordinary painting of Sir Ranald MacDonald of Staffa, sometime owner of the island, painted in full Highland garb, standing at the entrance to the cave.

Very few people have ever lived on Staffa. At its peak there were some fifteen souls in 1785. But since 1800 no one has inhabited the island. To dwell here would have been very tough, as there is hardly any running water and everywhere is exposed to violent storms and extremes of weather.

The shortest trip to Staffa is by boat from either Iona or Fionnphort. As Iona disappears, the passenger naturally turns towards islands further out to sea. Staffa appears as somewhat undistinguished, looming in the distance. But as the boat approaches it, the basalt columns and the extraordinary structure become apparent. Fingal's Cave and Boat Cave are prominent as black gaping holes in the cliffs; they lend an air of mystery and menace. Having skirted round Fingal's Cave the boat then parallels the outcrop of rock of Am Buchaille and, providing the tides are right, lands at the main landing point opposite Clamshell Cave.

Once you are on terra firma it is a short walk along what is known as the causeway over the hexagonal rocks to the famed Fingal's Cave, so named by Sir Joseph Banks in 1772 when people on Mull alerted him to its awesome nature. Prior to that it had always been known as the Melodious Cave. Perhaps musing on its original name inspired Mendelssohn to write his Hebrides Overture. The entrance is a mass of rock and swirling sea that rises up and down – sometimes green and sometimes azure. The cave itself penetrates deep into the island for some 230 feet/70 metres, culminating in a purple-tinged rock at its furthest point, where there is nothing but the sound of gurgling as the sea rolls back and forth. Outside, the restless waves crash against the bold upright 'staves' of rock that reminded the Vikings so much of home. This is what Sir Walter Scott meant by 'caverns of eternal thunder' in

BELOW Line of basalt rock on
Staffa, leading to Iona

RIGHT Am Buchaille, or the
Herdsman, on the approach
to Staffa

his poem 'Lord of the Isles'. Jules Verne called the cave
an enchanted place, conjuring up images of water nymphs.
From the causeway the eye follows the line of basalt rock
into the sea and thence directly to Dun I on Iona some 5
miles/8 kilometres distant.

Like many places in the world it is best to see Staffa
alone. The full experience can be had only without the chat-
tering of other visitors. It is also exciting to climb the steps
cut into the rock face and get on to the top of the island.
From the cliffs known as the Colonnade and the Great Face
you can appreciate the great expanse of the sea and look
down on Boat Cave. The volcanic Treshnish Isles and
Dutchman's Cap appear to be almost touchable and the
coast of Mull is well defined. From Mull, Staffa looks small
and isolated, at the mercy of the elements, until one sees
the strong upright staves of basalt.

There is an extraordinary connection between Mull,
Iona and Staffa through geography, geology and the lie of
peninsulas and hilltops. All are within sight of each other
at various points. Perhaps it is from the highest positions
of Staffa and Iona that one can really appreciate some of
the wilder aspects of Mull, where there are no roads or
houses, only waves crashing against the cliffs. Being on
Staffa and looking to Mull and Iona one can contemplate
the sheer longevity of these islands, represented by the
unique basalt rock formations. They fulfil the photographer
Henri Cartier-Bresson's dictum that 'landscapes repre-
sent eternity', for here on these islands certainly is that
deep feeling of eternity.

Clamshell coast,
above the landing
point on Staffa

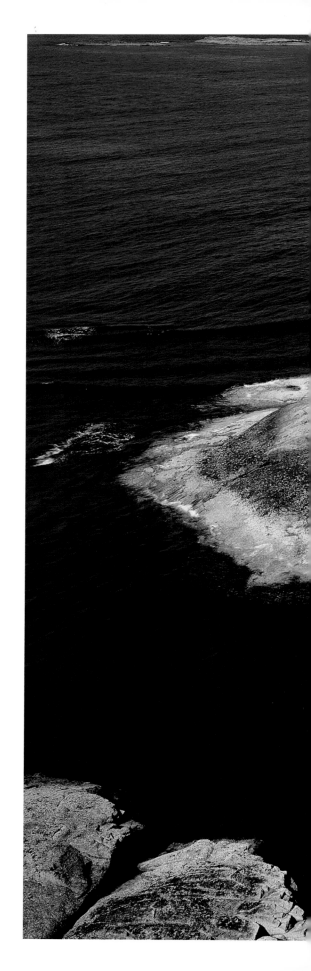

Photography Notes

Most of the photographs in this book were made using a large-format camera – that is to say, one that produces a transparency or negative 4 x 5 inches in size. It is known colloquially as a 45, or as a view camera. Where speed was of the essence or in high winds, I used a smaller Mamiya 7 rangefinder camera that produces a 6 x 7 centimetre photograph. Both cameras use film.

The view camera is always mounted on a tripod and demands a unique way of working. The process is contemplative and slow, and requires a good assessment of photographable locations. This suits me fine, for I work best once I get a good feel for an area or a particular landscape. On arrival, I may spend anything up to a couple of days looking at the ground trying to figure out how the light is falling across the landscape.

Critical to landscape photography is the vantage point or the point of view. Where the photographer sets up his tripod and camera is the first important step in achieving a successful photograph. That is why spending plenty of time on reconnaissance is important. Too often one hears the exclamation, 'I wish I had done that shot differently', which I have said myself many times, but possibly less frequently with experience. I have only four lenses, from wide-angle to short telephoto. Of those lenses I use mainly two – a wide-angle and a standard lens. I know how those lenses 'see', which helps me find the right vantage point.

The view camera sharpens the senses to the here and now of photography. This is because the image is seen through a glass screen on the back of the camera, which itself is the same size as the sheet of film inserted into its back – 4 x 5 inches. With the view camera every detail can be accounted for, and you have to take a good look at the elements of the composition. Waves or clouds can be seen moving across the screen, putting you right into the landscape. Using the camera is very absorbing but demands precision and concentration. View camera photographers look at detail; they grasp the interaction of shape and form and come to understand the relationship of the viewer to the subject. Perhaps photography represents not reality but 'the now' or the immediacy of the situation. A photograph can be made in anything from a split second to a number of minutes or longer, which is a pretty short space of time compared with other art such as a painting.

It is for the above reasons that I prefer to shoot film on a view camera rather than use a digital camera. To hold a transparency or a negative is like holding a stone, a blade of grass or grains of sand. To me it is real – it is an artefact. Unlike the digital image which is always viewed behind a computer screen. Having said that, there is no doubt that digital landscape photography has arrived and the quality is there, albeit at a price. That price has to be weighed up against the costs of purchasing film and processing it and transporting it. There are advantages of the digital format when travelling abroad given the ever tightening restrictions on baggage. Once in the field there are considerable savings in not having to man pack 40 sheets of film and film holders. Nor does one lose precious moments changing film. There are real advantages to seeing the image on screen as the photograph is made with perhaps greater scope for being more creative in the field. Ultimately it boils down to how the photographer likes to work and his approach to subject matter. The disciplines required of a view camera photographer will stand me in good stead should I make the switch to digital, which may not be far off.

Landscape photography like that in this book is about experiences in different places in all sorts of weather; of being alone with shapes, forms and moods created by light and atmosphere. The view camera enlivens those senses so that the photographer is ready – ready to be amazed and to be immersed in the mountains, or riverbanks, or the sea. If a location resonates a certain quality you respond, perhaps with awe in the case of a violent storm or with sympathy at the peaceful layout of some rocks.

Much of Scotland is undiscovered except by those who are intrepid enough to go looking. I cannot claim to have discovered Mull, Iona or Staffa, as many people come to these islands year in year out and know these places far better than I do. All I can do is offer my interpretation of them and, I hope, arouse curiosity in others, so that they too can experience that elusive Hebridean light and perhaps even have a go at photographing it themselves.

Bibliography

There are many accounts of Mull, Iona and Staffa, going back many years, even to Dean Munro in 1630. The journals of Dr Johnson and Mr Boswell in the late eighteenth century are lively and well known. Those authors did not pay much attention to the natural beauty of these places. It was only in the last 150 years and more recently that the idea of wilderness and pristine locations became part of our psyche to be revered rather than feared.

The following books are more contemporary and have fascinating insights into the history, folklore, culture and sights of Mull, Iona and Staffa.

Cornish, Joe, *Scotland's Coast*, 2005
Currie, Jo, *Mull: The Island and its People*, 2000
Gordon, Seton, *Hebridean Memories*, 1923
—, *Highways and Byways in the West Highlands*, 1934
Haswell-Smith, Hamish, *The Scottish Islands*, 2004
Holder, Geoff, *Mysterious Iona and Staffa*, 2007
Moffat, Alistair, *The Sea Kingdoms: The History of Celtic Britain and Ireland*, 2002
Murray, W.H., *The Islands of Western Scotland*, 1973

Acknowledgements

This book would have been difficult to complete without the help of a number of people who advised me on good locations and tried to understand my aims and what I was looking for. For this I would like to thank the following: Sir Lachlan Maclean of Duart and Morvern, Christopher James at Torosay, Richard de Klee, the staff at Finlay Ross on Iona and Mr Kirkpatrick, captain of *MB Iolaire* of Iona.

In Oban there is a photography gallery owned and run by Richard Childs with evocative photographs covering much of the west coast of Scotland and the islands. It is unusual to find galleries dedicated to photography and it is a gem. The gallery gets the mind into gear artistically, sowing creative seeds before you embark for the isles.

A book such as this is not produced without a considerable amount of help with administration and practical advice. For this the following have been of great assistance and I thank them all: Bruce Graham for tirelessly helping out at home with deliveries, computers, office work and repairs to equipment: Bruce Stannard and Susan Cromarty of Bowral, Australia, who have continued to display my photographs in their wonderful magazine *Scots*, and have a deep interest in and knowledge of all things Scottish; John Nicoll of Frances Lincoln for suggesting the idea in the first place and bearing with me during the making of this book; Ken Sethi and all at Genesis Laboratories in London for high-quality film processing; and above all Fiona, for unfailing good humour and encouragement during my absences in the Hebrides.

PREVIOUS PAGES Looking down on Am Buchaille, or the Herdsman, Staffa

RIGHT Storm approaching Scoor

FOLLOWING PAGES Run off into Calgary Bay

PAGE 112 Ben More and A' Chioch loom above Loch Scridain in a winter snow storm